POPULAR PET CARE

Fish

Ann Larkin Hansen
ABDO & Daughters

Pets are more than just a toy or a play thing. They are part of our families. It is important to love and care for them. Popular Pet Care will help you understand your pet and know of its unique needs. Remember that your pet will depend on you to be responsible in caring for it.

Dr. David C. Hallstrom—Veterinarian

JACKSON COUNTY LIBRARY SERVICES
MEDFORD OREGON 97501

Published by Abdo & Daughters, 4940 Viking Drive, Suite 622, Edina, Minnesota 55435.

Copyright © 1997 by Abdo Consulting Group, Inc., Pentagon Tower, P.O. Box 36036, Minneapolis, Minnesota 55435 USA. International copyrights reserved in all countries. No part of this book may be reproduced in any form without written permission from the publisher.

Printed in the United States.

Cover Photo credits: Vik Orenstein
Interior Photo credits: Vik Orenstein, Peter Arnold, Inc., Wildwood Studio, Super Stock, Connie Bickman
Illustrations and Icons by: C. Spencer Morris

Edited by Julie Berg
Contributing editor Dr. David C. Hallstrom—Veterinarian
Special Thanks to our Popular Pet Care kids:
Peter Dumdei, Gracie Hansen, Brandon Isakson, Laura Jones, Annie O'Leary,Peter Rengstorf, Morgan Roberts, and Tyler Wagner.

Library of Congress Cataloging-in-Publication Data

Hansen, Ann Larkin.
      Fish / by Ann Larkin Hansen.
      p.   cm. -- (Popular pet care)
      Includes index.
      Summary: Provides instructions for setting up and maintaining an aquarium and for caring and feeding the fish that will make it their home.
      ISBN 1-56239-782-6
      1. Aquarium fishes--Juvenile literature. 2. Aquariums--Juvenile literature. [1. Aquarium fishes. 2. Aquariums.] I. Title. II. Series: Hansen, Ann Larkin. Popular pet care.
      SF457.25.H36   1997
      639.34--dc21
                                                              97-1592
                                                                CIP
                                                                AC

Contents

What Is An Aquarium?

Have you ever wondered what it would be like to breathe and swim underwater like a fish?

Fish are quiet, beautiful pets. They take up hardly any space, and they don't mind if you have to leave them for a few days. They are fun and relaxing to watch.

Fish do need quite a bit of equipment, and you have to be regular with food and water changes. An **aquarium** is a big glass tank, full of water that lets you see how fish, snails, and underwater plants live. And an aquarium is usually the most interesting thing in a room!

A goldfish in an aquarium.

Equipment

Aquarium fish come from the warm, clean waters of the **tropics**. So, the aquarium water must be kept warm, clean, and moving. To do this, you will need a 10 or 20 gallon tank with a cover. The cover should have a light in it, and doors for feeding the fish. In the tank you will need a **filter** to clean the water, a **heater** to keep it warm, and an **air pump** to circulate and add **oxygen** to the water.

You will also need tubing to connect the pump to the filter, a fish net, a **siphon** tube, and a **thermometer**. You'll find just what you need at a pet shop. Many stores sell starter kits for aquarium beginners.

Opposite page:
Aquarium equipment.

Setting Up
Your Aquarium

First, decide where the tank will go. Since it will be very heavy, put it on something sturdy with plastic underneath in case of leaks. Don't put the **aquarium** in front of a window. The sun's heat would change the water temperature too much. Put the tank close to an electrical outlet, so you can plug in the **heater**, pump, and light. There should be space nearby to store fish food and the **air pump**.

Rinse the tank a couple times with warm water and set it in place. Put in the **filter**. An **undergravel filter** usually works best, and it lays on the bottom of the tank. Carefully rinse some medium-sized **gravel** from the pet store. Then lay it on top of the filter.

The **gravel** should be about three inches deep in the back of the tank, and about one inch deep in the front.

An empty aquarium is fun to fill.

Decorating Your Aquarium

Get some rocks or other **aquarium** decorations from the pet store. Many people tape a picture on the back of the tank to make it prettier. Rinse the decorations in warm water. Now put a small plate on the **gravel**, and slowly pour water onto the plate. This keeps the gravel from being stirred up. When the tank is half full, put the decorations around the sides and back. Leave room in the front for the fish to swim. Take the plate out and carefully finish filling the tank. Put in the **heater** and turn it on.

Fish use plants for food and hiding places. Try plastic plants first. Once you're good at keeping fish, you can try some live plants.

Make sure that you never use any soap or other cleaners in the **aquarium**. They could kill your fish. Also don't use any seashells or wood from outside. Rocks from a pond or stream can be used, but should be boiled before you put them in your tank.

Colored gravel makes your fish bowl nice and bright.

Adding Fish

Now comes the hardest part of all. You have to wait at least two days before you add fish to your tank. This allows time for any **chemicals** in the water to escape. Connect the pump to the **filter** with plastic tubing, and turn it on. Turn on the **heater**. Watch carefully to make sure everything is working properly. The water should stay at 78 degrees.

Finally it's time to choose your fish. You need fish that are tough and will get along with each other. Some of the best to start with are **guppies**, **tetras**, **platys** or moons, and **dwarf gourami**. Goldfish should not be kept with tropical fish.

Opposite page:
A Lion-headed
goldfish.

Bringing Fish Home

Choose fish that are healthy. They should be swimming well. They should not have ragged fins, dull eyes, or white spots.

The pet shop will put the fish in a plastic bag. Keep it warm and get home fast!

Float the bag on top of the **aquarium** water for about ten minutes. Then carefully open the bag and pour out a little water, then add some from your aquarium. Keep doing this slowly, until the bag is half full of water from your tank. Then you may turn the fish loose.

You can buy one inch of fish for every gallon of water. This means if you have a ten-gallon tank, you can have ten one-inch fish, or twenty half-inch fish.

Healthy fish swim well.

Algae and Scavengers

After a couple weeks, you will begin to notice a green film on the glass. This is **algae**. Algae is a small green plant that seems to grow everywhere that there is water. The fish like to nibble on it, but they can't keep it under control. It's time for **scavengers** to be added to the tank.

Scavengers are snails and fish that eat nothing but algae and **debris**. They keep the **aquarium** clean and the fish healthy. **Corydoras catfish** are good scavengers. Snails are too, but they multiply fast, and you need to take out the extras every month or so. You will still need to scrape or sponge the algae off the aquarium glass every week.

Your aquarium needs to be clean

Aquarium Chores

Every morning turn the light on and check the water temperature to make sure it's still 78 degrees. Fish need 12 to 14 hours of light every day, so you can leave the light on until you go to bed. Feed them flaked fish food once a day. Only give them as much as they can eat in five minutes. About once a week, give them freeze-dried tubifex worms from the pet store or a small piece of lettuce for a special treat.

You can buy a special **algae** scraper or just use a sponge when the tank starts looking green. Once every month, **siphon** off one-fifth of the water. Add new water that has sat for two days in a clean bowl. This is the most important **aquarium** chore.

**Feeding your fish
is important.**

Changing Water

Changing part of the **aquarium** water every month will keep your fish healthy. Be sure to turn off the **heater** before you start.

The easiest way to change water is with a **siphon**. This is just a piece of plastic tubing. Put it in the aquarium until it is completely full of water, with no air bubbles. Now put your thumb over one end, and put this end in a bucket on the floor. Keep the other end underwater. Take your thumb off. The water will flow into the bucket.

Use the end still in the aquarium like a vacuum cleaner on the tank bottom. When one-fifth of the water is gone, pull the siphon out of the tank. Isn't that a neat trick?

Changing water will help keep your fish healthy.

Keeping Fish Healthy

When fish get sick, they usually die. The important thing is to keep them from getting sick. Fish get sick usually for three reasons: too much food, too many fish in the tank, or too much temperature change. Crowding and overfeeding make the water dirty, and dirty water makes fish sick.

If a fish does get sick, put it in a jar that floats in the **aquarium**. This will keep other fish from catching the disease. Sometimes giving the fish a salt bath will help. Use a half teaspoon of salt in a quart of water, and put the fish in for ten minutes at a time. If all the fish are sick, give them a salt bath and change all the water in the aquarium.

Cleaning your aquarium is important.

When You're Not A Beginner Anymore

Once you've learned to keep fish happy and healthy, you may want to try even more interesting things. You could add live plants. You could try adding more difficult and beautiful fish.

Many **aquarium** owners learn to **breed** their fish so they will have babies. **Guppies** are the easiest to start with. Some people have **salt water aquariums** for ocean fish.

You can learn more from books, pet stores, and other aquarium owners. You may get hooked on aquariums for the rest of your life!

Opposite page: There are many different fish to choose from.

When Fish Die

Aquarium fish do not usually live very long. Anyone who keeps fish accepts that every so often one will die. A dead fish floats belly-up on the water surface, or lays on its side on the bottom. Pick it up with your net, wrap it in a plastic bag, and put it in the garbage. Then wash your hands.

Now you have to find out if the problem was the fish or the aquarium. Check the water temperature. Are the fish getting enough light, and the right amount of food? Is the water clean? Are the other fish showing signs of illness? If there are any problems, you need to fix them fast.

If everything else in the aquarium seems to be healthy and happy, the dead fish probably just died of old age. You can buy a new, young fish at the pet store.

Having fish can be a lot of fun.

GLOSSARY

Air Pump: A plug-in motor that pushes air through plastic tubing connected to the filter to add oxygen to the water.

Algae: Tiny green plants that grow on underwater surfaces.

Aquarium: A glass-sided tank for displaying underwater life.

Breed: Using male and female fish to produce babies.

Chemicals: Invisible substances in the water, such as calcium or ammonia.

Corydoras Catfish: A favorite scavenger fish for aquariums. Grows to about three inches. Use pellets that sink to the bottom to feed this fish.

Debris: Fish waste and other junk that gathers at the bottom of the tank.

Dwarf Gourami: Grows to two or three inches long. This fish is shy and needs hiding places.

Filter: A device that lets water through but stops particles and some chemicals.

Gravel: Small rocks that are about the same size. Available in many colors for aquariums.

Guppy: Colorful, active, and peaceful fish. They like plants to nibble on. They grow 1 to 2 inches.

Heater: A device that attaches to the top of the tank and hangs down into the water to keep the temperature constant.

Oxygen: A colorless, tasteless, odorless gas that forms about one fifth of the air and one third of the water.

Platy: Many different types of platies are available. They grow to 2 or 3 inches, and like lots of open swimming space.

Salt Water Aquarium: An aquarium that mimics ocean conditions.

Scavenger: Fish or snails that live mostly on algae and debris.

Siphon: A tube used to remove water from the tank, or the process of removing water with a tube.

Tetra: Small, active fish in many different colors. Beginners should start with neon or cardinal tetras. They grow to 1 or 2 inches.

Thermometer: A measuring device showing the temperature. Mount in the tank near the bottom.

Tropics: The part of the earth near the equator where temperatures and day length varies little during the year.

Undergravel Filter: Perforated plastic plates that fit on the bottom of the aquarium, with tubes rising up at the rear. This filter is almost invisible and probably takes the least care of any type of filter.

Index